"My review of **In**
ply delightful. I foun
digestible. Your subj
son can become connected. The presence of the Almighty, in your work, is what makes the difference for me.

I wish and pray for your success in this endeavor."

- H. Lewis Gillis
Thomas, Means & Gillis, P. C.,
Attorneys and Counselors at Law
Montgomery and Birmingham, Alabama

"Ms. Morris-Dotson's commitment to communicating her Christian faith and her love for people is demonstrated in this volume in a very interesting style of poetry. She has drawn upon Biblical events as well as her own life experiences to encourage and inspire a diverse sector of readers. Her Christian theology is sound, and her writing style reflects a gift which has been developed through education and practice of her faith.

It has been a pleasure for me as her former college advisor to have the opportunity to review her book of poetry as it reflects her development over the more than 20 years since she was my student."

-Kline W. Johnson, Ed. D.
Vice President Emeritus
Troy State University in Montgomery
Adult Sunday School Teacher
Eastern Hills Baptist Church - Montgomery, Alabama

"In the midst of the darkness...He is That Bright Light!"

In This World But Not Of This World

Different Enough To Make A Difference

Inspirational and Provocative Poetry by

Cynthia E. Morris-Dotson

CeSalAlve, Ltd.
Montgomery, Alabama
1997

In This World But Not Of This World:
Different Enough To Make A Difference,

For further information, please contact the publisher.

Publisher: CeSalAlve, Ltd.
P. O. Box 230863
Montgomery, AL 36123-0863

Library of Congress Catalog Card Number: 97-91929

Dotson, Cynthia E. Morris-
In this world but not of this world: different enough to make a difference/by Cynthia E. Morris-Dotson.
ISBN 0-9658508-0-3

First Edition

Printed in the USA by

3212 East Highway 30 • Kearney, NE 68847 • 1-800-650-7888

Foreword

As a young child, I dedicated my life to my God. In all that I do. . . I acknowledge, praise, and give honor and glory to My Lord, Who is the Head of my life.

My work is dedicated to my Maker as well. To God be all the glory. . . for only He is worthy to be praised!!

My Prayer of Dedication

Yesterday, today, tomorrow, and forevermore,
I give all praise, honor, and glory to my
God Almighty whom I truly love and adore . . .

Please inspire my thoughts Dear Lord,
please give me Your anointed words.
So that my message may exalt Your Holy name,
and will help to ease somebody's pain.

May my work glorify only Thy name Lord.
Please use me up to share Your blessed Word.
Please allow what You say through me
to become vivid and may it be, clearly heard.

Use me Lord, tell me what to say.
Please guide my mind and my heart, each and everyday.
Without You Father, I can do nothing,
as I write Dear Savior—let Your message ring.

Please allow the Holy Spirit to inspire every line,
and to Thee be the glory for we know it is Thine.
I'm only an instrument—to be used by You.
Teach me, lead and guide me Lord. Please show me what to do.

Let me boldly share Your words Dear Lord.
May Thy will be done, so it is You whom others see.
Let me decrease completely, and may You increase fully,
so that all exaltation, glory and honor may be to Thee.

I am Your servant Father. Use me as You wish.
And if I should find myself, oh Lord - in the belly of a fish,
please rescue me my Savior, from any whale or shark.
Please secure me in Your loving arms my Lord, as You did
Noah in the Ark.

Please use me Lord. Let me step out and walk by faith.
The words I share Dear Lord, let them be what Thy saith.

Amen.

Acknowledgments

I wish to express my sincere thanks to my family and friends, and to those whom I may have met from day to day, who listened attentively as I shared my thoughts and feelings. I pray that the shared words, thoughts and time were somehow inspiring and helpful to you as well as to others whom you have since met, and perhaps shared the same.

To my girlfriends: Jacintha, Ola, and Sadie; my dear niece and nephew, SoJuan Nichole and Willie Nathan, respectively; and my first cousin, Sara Louise - - thanks for listening and for the words of encouragement! Here it is! !

To my two beautiful and darling children, Adriane Leslie Virginia and Saint-Aaron Lennard Antwúan (the precocious one; your computer and photography skills are invaluable!) and to my precious little grandson, Adrian-LaBoderick Vaughn-Phillip... thanks for being such a treasured support system my precious ones. It is truly a blessing to know the love that we share. Remain honest and true to yourselves and be truthful to others. I thank God for you! Always remember to put God first, even before self, and He will forever keep "His songs in your hearts"!

Finally, to my mother, Mrs. Carrie Grayson Peavy, before the whole world — I want to tell you that "I love you Mother Dear".

Contents

A Servant of God

(I'm on the battlefield for my Lord,
I've received many wounds, but I haven't been destroyed)

I felt as though I was in a big black hole,
it was apparent to me that they wanted to steal my soul.
I was gradually losing all control,
but I held tight, and God strengthened my hold.

I was afraid, confused, and felt so all alone,
but in the midst of the darkness, I kept hearing a reassuring tone.
It was an open line of communication, better than any telephone,
it was the voice of my Lord, telling me "the job must be done."

So I smiled and wiped away my tears,
I waited for no applause, I expected no cheers,
I had grown accustomed to victories and heartaches over the years,
but my God Almighty always removed my fears.

I always talk with my Lord, and ask "What must I do?",
my Lord promised to guide me and see me through.
Sometimes I feel exhausted, dismayed, and blue,
And often I'm misunderstood by many — perhaps, even by you.

I just shake it off, and move on because I have my Lord's work to do,
and I can't give up, and will not be defeated — by a few.
"Lord", I ask, "what must I do?"
I am still waiting Lord, to hear from You.

We talk each day, and You have shown me too,
that You haven't finished with me yet. Lord I love You.

Don't let me give up,
please Lord fill my cup,
with Your precious grace and mercy as we sup.

I have been fed things that mess with my mind,
some of this stuff has clouded my vision, but I'm certainly not blind.
I can see the devil at work, and I say "Get thee behind,"
because my God is the Head of this line!

In fact, my God is in total and complete control,
and only my God owns my soul.
Therefore, I shall forever be bold,
because it is the Mighty Hand of God that I hold.

Actually, He holds me, He keeps me, and will never let go,
and I feel very much assured, for His Word tells me so.
If you study and hear His Word, you too will know.
When God says "Move", you must get up and go.

Step out on faith, knowing that He is the Light,
He will brighten your dark paths and lead you through the night.
He alone has all power — He alone has all might,
He will give you victory in your battles, so don't dare take flight.

Stand still and be of good courage,
and keep on God's armor,
as you fight a good fight.

Never take off His mighty armor of protection,
and you will be able to endure life's rejections.
You will stand steady as a rock, when any infection
attempts to weaken or destroy you, Christ will be the Reflection

that shows up in you.

And remember . . .
that you have,
God's work to do!
Please use me Lord.

A Song On My Heart

Jesus hung there on the cross, so that my soul would not be lost - because He loves me.
Jesus shed His precious blood, He never said a mumbling word - because He loves me.
He was brutally crucified, then He hung His head and died - because He loves me.
Jesus loves me, Jesus loves me - yes, Jesus really loves me!

The gift He gave to me, I know that it is free - because Jesus paid the full cost.
He bought it with His blood, He did it out of love - all because He loves me.
He paid the greatest fee, when He died for you and me - oh yes He loves me.
Jesus loves you and me, He died to set us free - way back on Calvary.

Jesus knows me by my name, He saved me from sin and shame - way back on Calvary.
I know He says it with a smile, when my Savior calls me His child - oh He loves me.
He adopted me as His very own, and now I never have to be alone - He watches over me.
Jesus loves me, Jesus loves me, yes Jesus truly loves me.

When I stumble and when I fall, to Him I always call - to rescue me.
He is always there on time, because I've got a direct line - He always answers me.
When I pray my Savior hears, He picks me up and dries my tears - because He cares for me.
Why don't you call Him up today, why don't you take some time and pray - let He hear from you.

He guides my path each day, and we talk along the way - He tells me what to do.
Jesus is all I'll ever need, and I'll follow as He leads - my footsteps each day.
Why don't you call Him up today, hear what our Savior has to say - He wants to hear from you.
Jesus loves both you and me, He died to set us free - way back on Calvary.

They pierced Him in His precious side, when He was crucified - I'm going to worship Him.
They whipped my blessed Lord, yet He never said a mumbling word - oh I'll worship Him.
Way back on Calvary, my Savior died to set us free - so let us worship Him.
Oh I'll worship Him, I'll worship Him - let us worship Him.

Only His shed blood would pay the cost, so our souls would not be lost - let us worship Him.
Jesus paid the ultimate price, when He lay down His precious life - so that we would be set free.
Because of sin man would be doomed, but Jesus lay in a borrowed tomb - then He rose again!
Oh He loves me, He loves me - and He has set me free!

When Jesus ascended into Heaven, there were now only eleven - disciples left.
And one of those had denied Him, before they crucified Him - still Jesus loved him.
And the dead one had betrayed Him, yet my Savior wanted to save Him - let us abide in Him.
A crown of thorns pierced His precious head, my Savior hung on that cross and bled - to set us free.
He died for you and me, He died to set us free - way back on Calvary.

They pierced Your precious side, You hung on that cross and died - way back on Calvary.
While there upon the cross, one thief's soul was not lost - because He called out to You.
My Savior gladly set him free, and no more a captive shall I be - because He died for me.
Oh I love Him, He set me free - way back on Calvary.

You lay down Your life for me, to redeem and set me free - oh how I love You.
They nailed Your hands and feet, but old death You did defeat - I've never doubted You.
I call on You night and day, and I hear You when You say - my child, I love you.
You have such amazing grace, no one will take Your place - I want to thank You.

Our lives have now been saved, for He did not stay in that cold grave - oh yes, He arose again!
The stone was rolled away, and Jesus arose on that third day - death could not keep Him down!
He gave us salvation from all sin, and now on Him I shall depend - oh how I love Him!
Oh Lord I'll praise You, I'll worship You - oh Lord I love You too!

He laid His hands upon my head, and then my Savior said - my child, I love you.
Each darkened path is made bright, and Jesus is that bright light - why not turn to Him.
Let Him guide you along the way, hear my Savior as He says - my child I'm here for you.
Completely trust Him, lean on His holy name - and He will protect and guide you too.

He placed His hand upon my heart, and from Him I won't depart
- Master, I really need You!
Sin caused darkness and made us blind, my Lord came down to
heal mankind - so that we might see.
Jesus Christ is the only way, can't you hear my Savior say -
come and follow me.
Dear Lord I love You, and wherever You abide - that's where I
want to be.

You suffered pain and agony, to set the captives free - sweet
Jesus, thank You.
You came down from on high, and was so willing to die - just for me.
They thought they had You bound, but old death couldn't keep
You down - and You arose again.
Because You love me, Yes Jesus loves me and He has set me free!

Oh death You did defeat, but even now it's not complete - for
You will return again.
And on that Judgment Day, we will hear our Father say - just
what the end will be.
So be careful how you treat, each and everyone that you meet -
along your way.
When Jesus examines your heart, would He be pleased - with
what He sees?

Please change my heart Dear Lord, let me abide in Thy Precious
Word - forever guide me.
With my blessed Lord I want to be, in Your Heavenly Home -
please welcome me.
Where you go I want to go, where You are I want to be - spending
eternity with Thee.
I'll worship You, I'll serve You - I want to spend all of my life with You.

Thank You Lord.

Amen.

An Examination of One's Sight and Heart

When he was bad,
he was really bad,
but when he was good,
he was even better!

You would not have wanted
to meet this man,
before he was blinded by the Master,
as he journeyed down that road to Damascus.

It was a walk
he was glad that he took.
For he was shaken,
I mean REALLY shook -
by the mighty hand,
of our blessed Lord!

The man was blinded,
all sight was gone!
For a moment this brutal warrior,
thought he was all alone.

He just didn't know,
what was in the plan,
because when his sight was restored,
he was truly a changed man!

Yes, old Saul was a killer of men.
He persecuted a multitude of Christians,
and was even present when they stoned Stephen.

But now he was commissioned,
to become a fisherman of men,
and he preached the Good News,
for all to turn away from sin.

He became a powerful preacher.
He was a devoted apostle and teacher.
Read God's Word - for it is written.
It has been revealed to us,
don't let it be hidden!

Allow your blindness to be cured by Jesus.
He is able to restore your sight.
Present to Him, your hardened heart.
Like Saul on the Damascus Road,
He wants us all to have a brand new start!

Go out yourselves, and share God's Word.
Don't be ashamed, let His message be heard.
For there are many who need to hear,
but don't be dismayed, if some have deaf ears.

The Lord will deal with each of us,
as He did with Saul - on the road to Damascus.
Yes he was blinded, but that's not all.
Oh yes, his name was changed from Saul to Paul!

That Damascus Road Experience

Let's get on that Damascus Road.
Let's give Jesus our heavy load.
He will open our eyes so we can see,
He will cleanse our hearts and set us free.

And when our hearts are changed,
by a new name, we will be called.
In His direction our hearts will nod,
because the name we will be given,
is a child of God!

So he who has ears, let him hear -
and with your eyes do see,
what our Lord has to offer to both you and me.
Open your hearts, and hear what He has to say.
Give Him your hearts and gladly obey.

For He has more to offer, so much more to give.
He offers salvation, eternal life - through Him you shall live.
For He is the Way, the Truth, and the Light.
You can come to Him, just as you are - any day or any night.

But don't wait! Don't hesitate!
For Christ is coming soon,
and you wouldn't want it to be too late!

He Is Awesome!

He is
Alpha
and Omega.

He is
The Beginning
and

He is
The End.

He is
The Starter
and

He is
The Finisher
and
EVERY VICTORY HE WINS!

My God is a Mountain Mover

David was only a small shepherd boy,
but a warrior giant he did defeat.
With a sling and one smooth stone,
he knocked Goliath, a giant, off his feet.

You see, it isn't the size of the problem,
and we should never fret with despair,
Because God is greater than any force,
just leave it all in God's care.

It really wasn't David's strength,
and the power was not in the stone.
The Power that brought Goliath down,
came from the One Who sits above
On His mighty throne!

Answer . . . "Yes Lord"

When God gives you work to do,
don't try to run, because you can't hide.
God will get your attention and your time,
even if He has to blind you, break you,
or let your problem cause you to be eaten alive.

I kid you not; this is true.
When it comes to God's Word I do not jive.

Just read His Word — for it is written.
Study the Word — it is not hidden.

Blinded Saul became Paul,
then he preached and taught God's Word, as he was called.

King Nebuchadnezzar was brought low,
and learned from that lesson, whom he should adore.

For three days and three nights, Jonah was housed in the belly of a whale.
After God let him out, he traveled to Nineveh to obediently tell
what God had directed him to preach.

Think on His Word, and His commands obey,
because when God tells you to speak,

God will tell you what to say!
Remember, He prepared Moses and Aaron before sending them to Egypt that day.

So don't think your mission in this world, is to be a self-serving task.
If you're not sure what God wants you to do, you only have to ask.

There is much work to be done, and God doesn't expect work from just a few.
God has something for everyone, and He has work for you to do.

Oh Lord, please speak to me!
Amen.

A Loving and Forgiving God

King David was a man of God.
He truly loved our Lord.
But one day David strayed away,
and lusted in his heart.

He watched Bathseba
as she took her bath.
Immediately David wanted her,
so he charted an evil path.

He sent for this woman,
and took her to his bed.
Yes, he knew that she was the wife of another man,
but David didn't think with his heart,
and not very well with his head.

Now more than before, for her David yearned.
This king seemed to have gone completely wild!
Very soon afterwards, Bathseba learned
that she was pregnant with David's child.

Now to prevent his sin from being revealed,
King David had Bathseba's husband, Uriah, killed.
Uriah died in battle, he was placed in the front line to die.
Yes, King David was mighty mighty desperate to cover his lie.

You see, lust can lead to lies
and lying is a sin.
And when you attempt to do battle with God,
you can never ever win!!

David sinned, and David lied.
God was not pleased, and that baby died.
David pleaded and he cried,
nevertheless, David and Bathseba's first child died.

David knew he had sinned, and did confess.
This king realized, that he had caused a mess.
David repented and was given a brand new start.
He is now know as, "a man after God's own heart".

David and Bathseba were blessed
with another son.
He became a very wise king -
his name was Solomon.

These men were wise,
but made mistakes, nonetheless.
But when we are faithful and obedient to God,
just trust Him - and He will do the rest.

God is Almighty and caring,
and He's forgiving too.
God loves all of His children . . .
God loves me, and He loves you!

Don't Ever Try to Graduate from God

I've often wondered why some of us
do not attend Sunday School.
Knowledge of God's Word,
is a very powerful tool.

Jesus quoted scripture,
when He was under attack.
When you abide in the Word,
and the Word abides in you,
You can shake the devil off your back.

Train up a child
in the way that he should he go,
and when he is older he will not depart.

But how do you expect
to have a successful ending,
if you didn't begin
with a proper start?

You never get too old for Sunday School,
it's for children and adults too.
Men, women, boys, and girls . . .
this message is for each of you.

I do not know how old you are.
The age to serve is not rated:
good, better, or best.

It is your obedience
to God's call,
that really sums up the test.

Therefore, I encourage you to study God's Word,
and talk to Him in prayer.
Attend church and Sunday School,
but then, don't you dare stop there!

Share His Word with family and friends,
and with strangers along the way.
Then put God's Word into practice,
as you live from day to day.

Be concerned for everyone,
Lord knows that Jesus is!
If one is lost, He searches to find,
because He wants us to be His.

Lean not unto thine own understanding,
seek the Lord while He might be found.
Hope to see you in Sunday School . . .

because in God's house,
in His Word,
in His bosom,
and in His presence,

is where I want to be found!

More of Christ

So you were watching the TV,
and what did you see?
Someone flashing a sporty new car,
or maybe in Hollywood, you saw another star.

The next thing you heard was, "be all you can be",
then you surfed through the channels for more to see.
You caught a glimpse of someone with a shiny sword,
but it was now getting late, and you were rather bored.

You started to reminiscence and thought about "Mike",
but you don't play ball as well, and you sure can't fight.
Then a voice, so sweet, reminded you that night,
of a wonderful glorious One whom you can be like.

He is forgiving, and loving, and ever so kind.
He died on Calvary for your sins and mine.
He hung on that cross for you and me.
Now, have you seen Him lately on TV?

Did you see him on the basketball courts?
Have you seen Him show up much, in any of the sports?
Did you see Him in many television ads?
Do you see Jesus in your moms and dads?

Well now, do you spend your time dreaming of success?
Just put Christ first, and give your best,
then step out on faith, and He'll do the rest.
With Jesus as a friend, you've got the very best!

So put away that remote control!
Give God some of your time; let Him have your soul!
Wherever you go, take the Lord with You,
and when trouble surrounds you, Christ will see you through.

If ever you're in a tight spot,
or out on a limb.
Remember, Jesus is better than any credit card,
and I DON'T LEAVE HOME, nor go any place WITHOUT HIM!

Be Like Christ

Have you examined your behavior today?

Based upon your mind,
your heart,
and your actions,

What do you believe our Savior would say?

Are your actions more like the persecutor named Saul,
or are you more like the Christian named Paul?

Do you try to hinder God's work,
or do you heed the Master's call?

Be mindful of what you think,
feel,
say,
and do.

Remember that God Almighty is omnipotent - He is all-powerful,
God Almighty is omnipresent - He is present everywhere
(at the same time),
God Almighty is omniscient - He is all knowing,
and God is aware of everything that you think,
feel,
say,
and do!!!

So let us be more loving,
and more forgiving too.

Let us be more Christ-like . .
is the message I wish to share with you.

Oh Listen to The Children Sing!

Oh listen to the children sing!
They lift their voices and let them ring.
Never missing a beat — Lord, how sweet,
to hear the children sing!

Thank God they have given their lives to You,
rather than turning to violent things to do.
And we must keep them on the right track;
teaching them to keep their eyes on You,
and never ever turn back!

Just keep singing children, and praying too,
that you are doing what God expects of You.
It may not seem like much — but do your best,
and remember dear children, God will do the rest.

Let us keep songs of praise on our lips — and prayer in our hearts.
Turn immediately to the Lord — get an early start!
For we know not the day nor the hour,
therefore, do not tarry for God has all power.
God can break you — then make you, into what He will have you
to be.
He has already paid the price — for both you and for me.

Don't hesitate — don't wait, until you think that you are ready.
Just reach out to the Lord — for His mighty hand is steady.
He will take you and protect you, with tender loving care.
Bring Him all of your burdens, and leave them there --
right at Our Savior's feet.

And keep singing those songs children, ever so sweet!
Sing solo, sing duet, sing quartet, or in the choir.
Wave and clap your hands—stomp and pat your feet!
When The Holy Spirit moves you, you will surely be on fire!
Oh listen to that melodious music—Lord, how sweet!

Yes, sing children sing.
Let your voices ring!
Sing to the Lord of Hosts!
Give Him your best,
give him more, and more.
Give Him the most!

Get up and move when you hear the Savior call.
And always remember,
Jesus paid it all!

Oh listen to the children sing.
They lift their voices and let them ring.
Never missing a beat — Lord, how sweet,
to hear God's children sing!

Sweet Dreams

Good night my son,
have pleasant dreams.
Stretch out and enjoy
your rest.

Your day was long,
and your journey in life
has just begun . . .
and tomorrow you will
face another test.

Your pencil and paper
lay neatly on the table.
I know that you are able,
and you are ready . . .
To do your very best.

So sleep and dream,
and enjoy your rest;
And then arise my son . . .
refreshed.

Then on tomorrow,
and everyday,
continue to do and give
your very very best!

Sweetness

Some roses are pink,
while sunflowers are yellow.
Juicy cherries are usually sweet,
and ripe pears are quite mellow.

Two Little Boys

(My Son and His Pal)

Oh what a day, what a day.
Our school is several blocks away
and we have to walk!
Oh well ole pal, what do you say?
Think of something—let's talk.

Hey man, look at that yard.
I'll bet that couple worked really hard,
keeping out all of those weeds,
and attending to all of those seeds.

Boy oh boy, what an awesome flower.
God did this you know — He's got great power!
Look over there, don't you see?
It's a big fat bumble bee!

It's busy making a "jar of honey".
Man, they sure make folks a lot of money.
Bumble bees help flowers to pollinate.
The male bee works together - with his lady mate.

My mother and father are teammates too.
Together there are lots of nice things they do.
Sometimes they each work alone.
When they are apart, they talk on the telephone.

The Lord we serve sure is great!
Look at all the fantastic things that He decided to create!

We've got our mothers and fathers, sisters and brothers.
And don't forget about aunts and uncles,
nieces and nephews, and grandfathers and grandmothers!

Yeah! There are great grands, and great-great grands,
and cousins,
by the dozens!

Man it's a blessing to have families, and friends
and good neighbors too.
And pals who are best buddies
just like me and you!

You know, this has been a pretty good walk
and a nice talk too.
Let's see. . . we've got our lunch,
our notebook, paper, and ruler.
Yelp, we've got everything.
Hey, it's fun walking to school with you!

Look, I see the school patrols ahead.
Hurry, let's catch up with the bunch!
Take care man,
and I'll see you at lunch!

The Duke

Son your dog takes early walks,
before we are even up.
I don't know what he is doing
but I hope it's not with another pup.

I heard you crying this morning,
you said "Daddy, daddy, wake up!"
You couldn't find "The Duke" anymore,
"The Duke" is my son's Cocker Spaniel pup.

Gee, I felt a bit of relief,
to have my yard to myself.
I was thinking of gardening again,
when I heard that your puppy had left.

However, in only a moment or two,
your dog had come home again.
It sure was nice to see you smile,
(but you should have seen me grin).

I know it wasn't kind for me to feel this way,
but your puppy's hair causes me to sneeze.
My eyes always itch and get full of tears.

However, it's not just your puppy that I'm allergic to,
I've acquired a number of allergies over the past few years.

Even though I smiled, a big wide grin,
I had feelings of sadness too.
You see, I have grown fond of your pup,
but I'm sure no one could love him as much as you do.
Because now, in addition to the three of us,
"The Duke" is family too!

And he wears my official stamp of approval,
because this dog has class!!!

Sweet Melodies

When I sing my heart feels less pain.
Sometimes I may laugh,
at times there may be tears.

But whatever sorrows were present,
none remain.
Because I talk it over with Jesus,
and I know that He hears.

Glory to Thee

Throughout the years,
My Savior has continued to wipe away my tears.

My God has kept me and watches over me from above,
He has comforted me and cradled me in his protective arms of love.

He has never allowed me to give up, nor drown in this sea of agony.
I am continually in His presence, and my Father constantly
sees about me.

Yes my Lord comes to see about me, and watches me from above.
I know He cares for me — it's reflected in His genuine and
undying love.

My Heavenly Father showers blessings and love upon me.
There is never a charge — it is abundant, and yes it is free!

I am God's child, and I know that He really really loves me.
Shout hallelujah, praise His Holy and Magnificent Name, sing
with jubilee.
Oh Lord, I thank You for all of Your love, and give all praise and
glory to Thee!

Sweet Music in the Air

My father sings tenor, and my mother does too.
My nephew and I sing, and do the best we can do.

Yes, my sister sings alto, in the gospel choir.
And when our family is at home, we sing together by the fire.

Lord my mother sings all over the house.
When she's cooking, while she showers, and in bed to her spouse.

Mother sings while she drives, and when she's a passenger in the car.
She sings on long trips and on short trips, no matter how far.

Mother sings when she's happy, and she sings when she is sad.
Mother sings in the sanctuary choir, standing right next to dad.

Yes, dad sings in the choir, and often sings solo.
One Sunday dad was leading a song, and wouldn't you know!

As dad lifted his voice and let it ring,
the Holy Spirit filled my Mother (so she asked dad for the mic),
and started to sing!

The congregation was rather surprised!
My heart was truly touched and tears began to fill my eyes.

Mother sang each note - she sang each part!
My mother sang straight from her heart!

Mother sang when she was a child even though she was shy.
Throughout her life, she has continued to sing
songs of praise to our Lord on high.

Many, many people love to sing.
So go right ahead, and let your voices ring,
with praises and thanksgiving to the King of kings!!

Unity

When I first met my husband to be,
I had no idea that we would become a family.
We first met singing in our church choir,
later that same year, we were sharing songs in front of the fire
(at my home).

I knew when he asked me to be his wife,
that I wanted to be with him for the rest of life.
Sometimes it is hard, so we continually pray,
and ask our Heavenly Father for guidance each day.

I know our marriage shall survive if it is *God's* will,
and when we want to give up, we will trust Him still.
We must learn to trust and obey,
and forget about trying to have our own way.

Happy is he who trusts in the Lord,
and leaneth not unto his own understanding.
We shall stand on His promises,
for when we stumble and fall,
we are apt to have a safer, happier, and more successful landing.

Soul Soothing

Singing does wonders for my heart each day.
Singing helps me along my way.
It helps me to deal with my sorrow.
Songs help me to smile and look forward to tomorrow.

Smile

When you are burdened, overwhelmed, and feel all alone,
just smile and remember . . .
Our Lord is able to cause obstacles, to become stepping stones.

If at times, people are mean and cruel,
just smile and remember . . .
God has the power to make any enemy, your very own footstool.

Put your trust in the Lord,
and you will learn other lessons.
He can take bad things, that were meant to hurt you,
and turn them into blessings!

He has turned so many mountains into miracles,
I know this to be true!
My Lord loves and protects His children . . .
call on His Holy Name - - He wants to hear from you!

It's Time to Invest

So give your share . . .

Make your deposit of . . .

Love,

Kindness,

Friendship . . .

Just Care!

These things will grow,
and you will receive
"Blessed Returns"!

My Grandmother Lifted Me Up

(In memory of Mrs. Carrie Louise Stewart Grayson, affectionately known as, "Mama Carrie")

My Grandma lifted me up,
she didn't teach me to be a fool.
My Grandma lifted me up,
she took me to church and Sunday School.
My grandma lifted me up,
she taught me the Golden Rule.

My grandma lifted me up,
sometimes she would send me to town.
My grandma lifted me up,
she taught me not to mess around.
My grandma lifted me up,
and I hope I haven't let her down.

Mama Carrie you lifted me up,
and I want to thank you for everything.
You shared God's Word with me at a very tender age,
and every since with my lips and with my heart
I have been able to sing
praises to our King,

Whom you lifted up
and directed me to do the same.
Mama Carrie,
when my heart was sad,
you shared His Word,
and today His Word
still lifts me up.

Thank you for everything,
You were a great and wonderful grandmother.
You made a remarkable difference in my life I must say,
You touched so many lives along the way.

You gave so much of yourself to others.
You were a very dear friend and a great and grand mother.
I shall never forget that day,
when I arrived and stood at your bedside, and then you
passed away.

I love you Mama Carrie.
Although you have "gone on", I still love you!
I shall always love you dearly!

To God Be The Glory

"Great day, the righteous marching,
great day, God's gonna build up the
zion wall" . . . the voices of the gospel choir ring.

Then in a strong and melodious voice,
the congregation listens as Mama Jeanie sings
praises to our Lord above,
she does it with such devoted love.

Her voice is strong and distinct,
as she sings each note with such sweet succinct.
God filled sweetness, and humble meekness,
she bellows out praises to our God,
and I feel the Holy Spirit stirring within my heart.

My feet started to pat as I sat in the pew,
then others joined in and I certainly knew,
that the sweet, sweet Spirit was in this place,
as the patting and the clapping continued it's pace.

My hands started to wave,
because I know that I've been saved,
and I couldn't hold my peace as I started to moan.
I had to let the world know that I'm never alone,
and the joy that I feel you can too,
if you invite Jesus in, He will come in and sup with you.

You will be filled with the Holy Ghost Power,
and will feel Him dwelling in you hour after hour,
day by day --
as you walk, as you talk,
as you sing, and as you pray.

Yes, Mama Jeanie puts her soul into
this wonderful singing that she loves to do.
I thank God that she shares her gift with me and with you,
as she continues to sing praises to our Lord above,
Yes Mama Jeanie sings out of love,
for the Mighty God whom she has chosen to serve.

It is His Precious Name that we must glorify,
from this very day, and until the day that we die,
and then continue in the sweet by and by,
as we join our Father in our home on high.
It is Thy Holy Name alone, Dear Lord, that we glorify!!!

The Greatest Joy

Joy, Joy, God's great joy!
Not my joy, not your joy,
but God's great joy is deep down in my soul!

And it rises above all circumstances in life.
It carries me through heartaches, tribulations, and strife.

This world didn't give this joy to me.
Jesus paid the price, and I'm so glad that it's free!

Because if mankind was in charge,
I'm sure that his fee would be too large.

It would be a price that we could not pay,
and we would be without happiness everyday.

And every single night,
would be filled with darkness.
We would be without light.

But King Jesus is the Light of this dark world.
He is my Savior, He's my all and all.
He is more precious than any pearl!

The earth is the Lord's, and the fullness therein,
He's given me unspeakable joy,
because He died for our sins.

So how can the world possibly take away,
what the world cannot give?
My sinful debt Jesus chose to pay,
when He gave His precious life that day.
And today, right now, my Savior lives.

So I sing songs of praise, because I have been set free.
Yes, my Savior died, rose again, and lives for you and for me.

I have joy down in the depths of my soul,
because the precious blood of Jesus
has made me whole.

The Most Precious Gift

Jesus didn't lose His life on the cross.
Jesus gave His precious life
so that our souls would not be lost.

He paid the full price,
to free us from the bondage of sin.
So why not open your hearts,
and allow Jesus to come on in.

Jesus wants us to be His very own,
so that we will never ever have to be alone.

Jesus paid it all, and didn't charge us a cent.
Later He ascended into Heaven,
and the Holy Spirit was sent,
to abide within the hearts
of those who choose to repent.

He is here for all of mankind,
so open your eyes and stop being blind.
Blinded by the trinkets of lustful sin.

Just let go of the worthless treasures of this world,
and let King Jesus become your Savior and Lord.
Let a true friend come in — abide in His Holy Word.

Have Not and Wanna Be

None of us have led perfect lives,
we all have blemishes and spots.

So why do some of us, mistreat and label people,
as if some are the "haves",
and others are the "have nots"?

If you think for a minute,
that you can take earthly possessions,
away from this earth when you die.

Then you are really truly
fooling yourself.
You'll know the truth,
by and by.

Now about the "wanna bes",
and the "haves",
and for those who may think
they "have not".

If you have acquired worldly possessions-
by whatever the means-
but don't have Jesus,
then you are still,
a "have not"!

And if you don't have Jesus,
please call yourself a "wanna be",
because I "wanna be", with Jesus-right now (always),
and forever in eternity.

Jesus is the only One,
without a blemish or a spot.
And when you give your life to Jesus Christ,
you then will have a whole lot!

You will actually have all
that you will ever need.
No one owns Jesus,
He doesn't come with a lien nor a deed.

You really don't have a thing yourself,
none of this you really own.
Even your time here on earth is borrowed,
but "Salvation is a gift from Jesus - Salvation is not a loan"!

Let Jesus Come In

Sure I knew that in the "game of life",
there would be agonies, pain and strife.
I was out on the field — dead in the center.
I thought I was "a part of the team" — perhaps, even a winner.

One day the door opened, and I sure didn't want him to enter -
for I knew he would throw me a curve.
I tried to be steady,
but I just wasn't ready,
and sure enough, old Satan got on my very last nerve!

You can't become too sure,
of just how much you can endure.
But when the going gets to you;
lean and depend on the One who is true.

He is a friend who will stick by your side.
He will pick you up, and will be your guide.
So don't ever let the devil divide you!
Don't ever allow the devil to ride you!

Just shake it off, pack it under, and keep getting up.
And when Jesus knocks on your door, allow Him to come in and sup!

It Wasn't my Choice . . .

I had been made a "grande" at a very young age.
this made me furious — I was in a rage!

My daughter was away, attending college,
and I had just returned to the "States" when I received knowledge,
that she was expecting a child.
I tell you the truth, I nearly went wild.

After talking with her, I started to tremble
for her pregnancy started to resemble
what I had to face — all the shame and disgrace.
I couldn't stand anything that caused me to reflect,
on a painful past I wanted no one to detect.

Her having a child or children is what I had feared,
for my mind had already been "programmed and geared",
to love my daughter in a "bitter/sweet" way.
It is a problem that I continue to wrestle with, even today.

No one can image what we have gone through,
it can't be conceptualized unless it happened to you.

It was a dark cloud — it was a heavy drape,
that passed over me, and constantly covered me --
the day that I became a victim of rape,

As a result, my daughter was born,
from that day until now, my heart has been torn!

But because of the power of God above,
I am more secure, due to His unconditional love.
I've gained renewed strength from His amazing grace,
and though my heart is still healing, I now have a happier face.

So today, when I'm out and people ask,
"Who is the little one?",
I proudly reply, "He is my grandson!"

Victimized

Why are victims — victimized?
Why do some families, friends, communities, and institutions.
create lies?
Why do we hide our shame?
Why are we expected to hide others' shame?
Why are there sometimes
"cover ups?"

Why do "they" prance around with silly grins?
While we hurt deep within,
and are expected to forget.

How can we forget . . .
pain that has never been acknowledged,
issues which have not been addressed?

No one has sought to resolve
the pain,
the memories,
the nightmares,
the agony,

the invasion of our person,
the invasion of our space,
the invasion of our place,
the invasion of our very existence.

It was the wrongful invasion
of my body!!!

It was the heinous
violation of me!!!!

It's Like This

I do not fear death,
but I do detest pain.
So please don't hurt me!

Sheltered

Often I lay awake
on sleepless nights,
and oh how I have cried!

There were no friends
whom I trusted enough,
nor a family member
in whom I could confide.

I soon came to know and trust,
a Greater and Higher Power.
One Who has never deserted me,
and Who has comforted me in my darkest hour.

This Great Power
comes from above.
He fills my heart with joy,
and showers me with His love.

No one nor anything,
will ever take His place.
I am strengthened and renewed,
and I am saved by His loving grace.

Always my Lord
watches over me.

My Silent Prayer

Forgive and forget.
I haven't come to that conclusion yet.

For I am angry still,
at your violent intrusion
and your going against my will!

You hurt me you know.
But you don't even show
any sign of remorse or shame!

I have suffered for years,
and have shed countless tears,
and I have endured great agony and pain!

I have fervently prayed to my God,
and asked that He will guide my heart
to forgive, and allow me to let go.

He has placed abundant joy in my life!

Now I march to a different beat.
The music that I hear is ever so sweet,
and the voice that I hear with my ears, my heart, and my mind,
is the voice of my Lord. It is reassuring, gentle, and kind.

It soothes my woes,
and I have peace of mind.

Now I can forgive, and press on "His way."
For I look forward
to a much "brighter day,"

in the sweet by and by.
when I shall reside, with my blessed Lord,
in my heavenly home on high.

Thank You Lord, for Your loving kindness.
Thank You, for allowing me to be Your witness!

When I come to Your altar in prayer,
I am thankful to be able, to leave my burdens in Your care!

Life

I've always enjoyed
playing golf and tennis.
Those games to me,
are together, classy, and cool.

But when you get on the course,
or on the court.
Be a good sport . . .
after all you don't want to be caught
looking nor acting . . .
like a fool.

Whether it be golf, tennis,
or any other game in life.
You must learn and follow the rules.
You must study, work and practice
with all the proper tools.

The first step should be forward.
Work hard, play hard,
be honest and true.
Do unto others,
as you would have others,
to do unto you.

Slow down if you must,
rest for awhile
but never ever quit!
Keep prayer in your heart,
God on your mind,
and your eye on the prize.

And before the day is done,
and before this life is over . . .
hopefully you will realize.

That life is not a game,
and no game in life,
should come before SERVING THE LORD!

My Joy Cometh from the Lord!

Joy, joy, God's great joy!
Not my joy — not your joy,
but God's great joy fills me to the depths of my very soul!

It rises above all circumstances in life.
It carries me through heartaches, tribulation, and strife.

This world didn't give this joy to me.
Jesus paid the full price, and I'm so glad that it is free,
because if mankind was in charge,
I'm sure that his fee would be too large.

It would be a price that we could not pay,
and we would be without happiness each and everyday,
and every single night,
would be filled with utter darkness.
We would be without any light.

Thank God that King Jesus is the Light of this world.
He is my Savior — He is my All and All!
Yes, my Jesus is more precious than any pearl!
The earth is the Lord's, and the fullness therein.
He's given me immeasurable joy, because He died for my sin.

So how can the world possibly take away,
what the world cannot give?
My sin debt, Jesus chose to pay,
when He gave His precious life on Calvary Hill.
And today, right now, my Savior still lives!

So I sing because I'm exceedingly happy; yes, I have been set free.
Because my Savior died, rose again and lives for you and for me.

I now have joy way down deep in my soul,
because Jesus' blood has cleansed and made me whole.
You talk about joy! Oh my God's great and wonderful joy is deep within my soul!!!

Let's Share . . . The Good News

Have you contacted friends, to share some news
that you thought somehow might please us?
Well, if you want to talk about a friend,
and want to talk to a real friend —
then begin talking about, and try talking with
a genuine friend — His name is KING JESUS!

If your head feels dizzy
and you just want to get busy -
be about the business of the Lord.
Don't get into mess - get into His Word.
There you will find peace and happiness,
and will reap a much greater reward!

So if you want to get into somebody's business -
be about the business of the Lord.
If you want to "share the news" share the *Good* News!
"Spread the Gospel" — not gossip.
Let's talk about King Jesus — let us BE A WITNESS!

Rectified

So many "messed up people",
keep "messing" with people,
causing this "messed up world",
to be an even bigger "mess".

Get" right".
Do right.
Treat others right.
So what is wrong,
will be made right.

Let's RECTIFY the situation!

Let's Make It Better

Wouldn't it be nice,
if people were nicer?

Wouldn't the noise sound better,
if it was much lower?

Wouldn't it be much safer on the highways,
if we were more courteous, and drove a bit slower?

Do you think we might hear each other better,
if we didn't shout so loud, or scream and yell?

Perhaps, gossip wouldn't exist,
if we didn't tell

that which wasn't worth repeating in the first place.

Can't we be more cooperative?
More thoughtful?
More patient?
A bit kinder?
More responsible?

For in this "RACE", we are all HUMAN
and belong.
So let's just TRY HARDER
TO GET ALONG!

Have a Super Day!!

Do you have this,
or does it have you?

There are some who aren't able,
but if you are, don't fall for the label.

You have two eyes, and are able to see,
two ears, you say, are a part of me.

With them both, or at least with one,
you can hear most, and if not all, at least some
of what is said.

And you still have a head . . .
with which you can think, and a mind
with which you can dream.

You have two, or at least one arm,
and one, or both legs, and feet.
Well, that makes a pretty good team!

You have a mouth and a voice,
or at least some device to help you talk.

You've got legs, or maybe wheels
to help you to walk.

You are still "able",
or at least you can feel
some hurt and pain.

And if you are with me
(so far),
then you are not that "insane".

You can still breathe,
or at least you can sigh.
Well that should cause you to realize,
that you haven't said your last goodbye.

Your hair may be gone,
and your teeth may be too.
So what the heck!
Buy some more --
just as good and brand new!

Get rid of that frown.
It's not attractive, and certainly not in style!
Laugh, grin, chuckle,
hey, there's that lovely smile!

So everything hasn't gone your way!
Just be thankful with what you've got,
and Have a Super Day! !

Family

You are my child,
I am your mother,
this is your sister,
who is your brother?

I can see the wonder
in your eyes,
so listen son,
without surprise.

Be loving and kind
to your family, friends, and others,
for in the eyes of God,
we are all sisters and brothers!

Assurance

I will trust in the Lord,
and never despair.
When trouble is upon me,
I shall leave it all In God's Care.

For Real

Before some people will go outside,
their true identify they try to hide.
They won't show who they really are - on the inside.
Is it insecurity, that they somehow confuse with pride?

They don't feel at ease with who they are.
They want to look perfect — while hiding that scar.
They park around the corner, because they are ashamed of their car.
Some people just won't accept who they really are!

Don't let some people gain that extra inch.
They will squeeze into those girdles, no matter how awful the pinch.
They turn up their noses as if they smell a stench,
and in their own backyards is the foul trench.

Some people will have little or nothing to do with you.
They make premature judgments, without even a clue.
And if you walk on their grass, they are ready to sue.
And in church, they claim their very own pew.

Within these lines, maybe there is a clue,
of someone whom you've met,
or perhaps, it applies — to even you!

Roll Call

Some people do with supposedly good intentions,
then gather together a large crowd,
and make sure what they have done is mentioned.

Some want to be roasted and toasted,
and held in high esteem.
Their very own praises and glory they sing.

We are to praise God Almighty,
and glorify only His Holy name.
You know it's true, some of us have no shame!

Some want awards and plaques,
certificates, and ribbons,
and this and that.

Some want their names and faces,
in bright lights, in halls of fame,
on monuments and shrines,
on walls, on buildings,
on streets and signs.

Many are racing to reach their goal,
but how many are striving to be -
on our Creator's honor roll?

Cowards and Fools

They thought . . .
and thought. . .
and thought. . .
but took no action,

Then others acted,
without thinking.

Both groups resulted in total disaster!
Allow neither to become your master,

For they are both useless tools.
I'm speaking of none other than — "cowards and fools".

Attitude Adjustment

Don't focus on your
dis-ability,
but rather
on
His-ability.

For truly HE IS ABLE!!

Do Something!

So you wanted to be a "legal eagle",
and then your mind went blank.
Don't get discouraged, you can still "use your tank!"

You may not prepare briefs, or oversee judicial cases,
but one thing for sure,
if you are reading or hearing this poem,
you're not quite "pushing up daisies!"

So take your pen in hand,
and try to "think big!"
Write stories, write poetry,
get another "gig!"

If you don't want to cook,
get out of the kitchen.
Take a jog in the park -
heck, go fishing,
for a new niche in life!

You've still got some time left yet,
(none us know how much).
But before you leave, give something back,
do so-and-so, and this-and-that;
do whatever you can, to help with the debt.

So you too, have run across
some "bumps in the road?"
well don't just sit there grumbling,
and adding to the load.

Just shake it off, pack it under
and rise above the situation.
Don't you dare try to cruise through life,
as if it's just a long and paid vacation!

Turn to the left, turn to the right,
and make a very good choice.
If you can't use your hands,
perhaps, you can use your voice.

But don't sing songs of defeat.
Use your head, use your eyes,
use your hands, and use your feet.
Just use whatever you have and continue on,
until the journey is over, and the victory is won!

Life is much too precious
So don't take a life — don't waste a life,
neither yours — nor another's.
Why not share your wonderful and precious life with others!

Bank on It

Charge nothing,
And without expectation,
Receive much.
Express God's love.

CARE!

Sure You Have!

Have you ever been down to your last dollar,
and didn't have enough money - to buy enough to swallow?

Sure you have!

Have you ever gone to the kitchen to get a bite to eat,
only to find "leftovers of leftovers" — a "food repeat"?

Sure you have!

So what do you do besides look for a coupon?
You look under soft drink bottle tops - to see if you have won!

Sure you have!

You were hoping to get a free soft drink - to go with your snack,
to ease those stomach pains - and stop that hunger attack.

Sure you have!

Some of us have been there.
But if you ask some folks, they might swear,
"I have only known wealth!"

Sure you have!

Honey, don't buy that - they are only fooling "self".
However, you made it anyway - but not alone.
God always provided a way, because you could have been gone!

Thank You Lord, for Your loving kindness.
Thank You Dear Lord, for seeing me through all my distress.

Because I know that - "You sure have!"

We Are Our Brother's Keeper

Some will become homeless,
while some will have more homes than they will ever need.

Some will grow old, become sick and lonely,
while others will not make it from their mother's womb.

Some will be warriors — others peacemakers,
while some will be healers—others will be killers.

Some will be penniless — poor and without.
while others will have wealth untold.

Some will have little,
yet will talk about it a lot.

Some will be builders — others will destroy.
Yet, some will only scheme and plot.

Some will be creative and artistic,
while others will be destructive and unrealistic.

Some will educate — some will legislate,
while some will minister to others' needs.

Some will organize — some will create chaos,
while some will hurt others, and do bad deeds.

Some will be truthful — some will tell lies,
while others will rely on alibis.

Some will build themselves up,
while some will lift up others.

Some will give up their life for another,
while others will kill their own mother,
father, sister and brother.

Some will judge — some will defend.
Some will be honest — while others will pretend.

Some will speak out — some will keep quiet.
Some will stand up for truth — and others will run and hide.

Some will share a smile or a hug,
while some will frown and glare,
and others will push, pull and tug.

Some will give — some will take.
Some will mend — while others break.

Some will brag — some will boast.
Some will celebrate and make various toasts.

Some will work — some will play.
Some will share with others — while others will only take.

Some will break the peace - starting rumors and wars,
while others will placate.

Just know that God is watching from on high.
He knows our hearts, and He hears and sees all that we do.
And now I ask my brothers and sisters,
"Just which one are you?"

Questions???

Were you ever penalized
based on someone's misconception?

Did you ever trust the "wrong" person
due to deception?

Have you made an unwise choice
based on a faulty perception?

Were you ever a part of an inception
and later became the exception?

Stated. . . Slated

Psychotic,
neurotic,
erotic . . .

Exotic
names,
to proclaim . . .

the sanity
and the vanity

of the mind,
body,
and
spirit.

Think!

Have you ever been ostracized . . .
for being different,
because you refused to go along to get along,
because you created waves,
because you effected change,
because you a made a difference,
because you spoke up,
because you spoke out,
because you stood up,
because you stood out,
because you wouldn't back down,
because you wouldn't shut up,
because you wouldn't put up
(with "crap"),
because you wouldn't put out
(oh yes, you know),

So you are different!
Dare to be,
Different enough to make a positive difference!!

Crisises

Have you ever been...

Victimized,
criticized,
minimized,
penalized,
emphasized,
actualized,
polarized,
socialized,
notarized,
legalized,
ostracized,
jeopardized,

or wrongly advised,
then realized,

no one would help,
no one seemed to care,
no one would listen,
no one wanted to "get involved,"
no one had the time?

You learned,
that there was no concern,
because no one considered it "their problem."

Few, if any, were interested . . .
because no one wanted to "make waves,"
because they just wanted to "go along - to get along,"
because it didn't affect them,

because they didn't see anything in it for them,
because they've "got theirs - now you get yours,"
because they feel that "it can't be that bad,"
because they just "don't want to 'touch' that,"
because they feel that "it be's that way sometimes."

Get involved!
Be a risk-taker!
Stick your neck out!
Have some guts!
Take a stand!

Speak up!
Speak out!

Have faith!
Have courage!
and
(Exercise both!!)

This isn't just a poem,
nor only an inference.

I'm speaking to you!
To those who dare;

I'm sharing this message,
perhaps you care,
to be . . .

"Different Enough to Make a Difference!!"

Have You Given Lately?

God
Gave
His
Only
Begotten
son.

What have you given today?

Speaking of Green

Grass is green,
and money is too.
Your Child Support payment,
is long OVERDUE!!

Hard Lessons Learned

Some people have never learned,
perhaps, that's why they get "burned".

Don't you know yet,
or did you forget?

If it's not your money,
don't spend it!

If it's not your bed,
don't get in it!

Illegal money,
and illegal sex,

will be your downfall - everytime!

And you can take that -
to the bank
(if it's yours),

or go to jail,
(if it's mine)!

Tears

They cried tears
they tried to hide their tears.
then they dried their tears.

Then they laughed themselves to tears,
because of the reason
that they were crying.

Perhaps justifiable,
maybe not.
Some may cry a little,
while others may cry a lot.

People may not understand
why they or others cry,
But I have shed countless tears,
and crying has been good for my soul.

Thank You Very Much!

If you don't want to hear my cry,
don't cause me pain.
Stop hurting me!

What's Your Point?

Pardon?
Say what!

If you are "trying" to tell me
something,

I will understand you better,
if you would
"just say it!"

Who's Fooling Who

Mr. and Mrs.
sit holding hands,
she's faking it --
trying to protect her man.

He sits there stiffly --
afraid to look around,
thinking his eyes might meet,
one of "his women" in town.

He's afraid to leave,
claiming, "she'll get everything".
So he's faking it too,
as he nervously twists his wedding ring.

This has gone on -- day after day,
and now for several years.
They have yelled and fought,
and shed many bitter tears.

Neither will leave — for they are concerned,
with what people will say.
And even though both are miserable,
they both continue to stay.

He and one of his "lovers",
now have a child together.
And of course, his wife feels threatened,
fearing that he will leave her.

The law requires this father,
to provide his child support.
It sure is a shame that he refused,
and thus, had to be taken to court.

Oh what pain and grief we bear,
when we fail to kneel daily in prayer.

Marriage and Divorce

They tied the knot,
then knotted ties.
Got tied up in knots,
then said their goodbyes.

Reflections

A quick glance,
a warm smile,
a gentle touch,
a welcomed embrace ...

cause my eyes to glisten,
my heart to leap,
my skin to tingle,
my face to blush,

each time I choose to remember
when we were together.

Stubbornness

So you're gone . . .
Goodbye, so long!

Well, don't just stand there.
Leave with dignity, not in despair.

Oh, now are you saying that you do care,
and leaving this way just doesn't seem fair?

Are you waiting for me to express my sorrow?
Perhaps you should sit for awhile,
or come back on tomorrow.

Neither of us wants to admit our fault,
nonetheless, this matter has brought our relationship to a halt.

Isn't it a doggone shame,
that we wear our pride as if it were our fame?

Oh, I do love you with all of my heart;
and I hurt, and miss you so very much whenever we are apart!

Yet, this foolish pride stands in our way,
and prevents us from sharing what we really wish to say.

If you won't say "I'm sorry", and "I love you", then maybe I should;
and if I wasn't full of such selfish pride — without hesitation, I would.

Suddenly, I remember that I am in Christ and Christ is in me!
It is then that I recognize, almost immediately,
without a doubt, that I can!

Within that moment, I gently take your hand.

I look into your eyes, and with a gentle smile
I tell you that I'm sorry, and
that I love you.

And all the other wonderful
feelings in my heart
and my head,
that I want to express
and share
with you,
just might
take awhile.

So we sit and talk and pray,
and with hope and great courage . . .
we look forward to yet another
blessed day!

(To fathers and sons, mothers and daughters, sisters and brothers, husbands and wives, lovers and friends, to classmates and playmates, neighbors and co-workers, politicians, churches (body of Christ), and fellow countrymen . . . it's time to make amends)!

Humbleness

When you are mistreated, just pray to God
and turn the other cheek.
Don't become enraged,
instead, be humble and meek.

Whenever someone harms you,
don't seek to return them hurt.
Why not try being gentle and kind,
this will put them and others on alert.

This reflects great strength, indeed,
even if you may appear to be weak.
Remember, our Father has for you a great reward,
just pray and trust our Savior and Lord.

And to the ones who are causing pain,
you really ought to be ashamed.
You certainly need to stop hurting others,
and quit finding fault and blame.
Try spending some time on bended knees,
and begin calling on our Savior's name.

Be kinder to your sisters and brothers,
rather than always lashing out at others.
Stop calling people out of their names,
and call on the name of the Lord.
Quit trying to hold others down,
and help them up by applying His Word.

Instead of raising your hands to hurt others,
try reaching out for the hand of the Lord.
Let us love one another,
and stay on one accord.

Confidence

My heart is glad,
even when
I feel somewhat sad.

And doing hours
of sorrow and distress;
deep within I have peace
and happiness.

Because my Lord is in control . . .
yesterday,
today,
and tomorrow
are His to hold!

Let's Not Hurt Each Other

It hurts me
when I hurt you.

It hurts me
when I'm hurt
by you.

So let's not hurt each other!

A Request from the Heart

I do not fear death,
however I do not like pain.
So until my Lord calls me home,
could you please not hurt me so much?

Just In Case

I don't avoid fire hydrants,
neither am I afraid to stand
between a dog and a tree.

However, I do wear
protective armor,
so no one will "pee" on me.

(A risk taker . . . not a fool!)

Different

Where is it written
that I must write
like you,
or that you must sing
like me.

Why can't we write
and sing
our very own way,
and be
differently.

This is My Prayer

Oh Heavenly Father,
as I begin yet another new and glorious day,
and as I continue along Thy blessed way,
please guide my mind, my heart, and my steps
as I travel oh Lord, I pray.

Dear Master,
please bless my efforts and cause my work.
to exalt and magnify Thy wondrous name.
Oh Lord, please use me to Thy glory.
I pray that You will be in everything
that I do. I want to be used by you.

My Savior wherever You lead me,
please cause me to obediently follow Thee.
I don't ever want to be away from Thy presence Dear Lord.
Wherever You go, that is where I want to be.
I pray that what I say will be pleasing to You.
I pray that my work, as expressed and shared,
will be inspiring to others, and helpful too.

I pray Dear Master, that You alone, will be lifted up.
I pray that You and only You will be honored and praised.
Please use me Lord to tell others of Your amazing grace.

Please let some aching heart be soothed by what You tell me to say.
Please let some lost soul be found along the way.
Please allow some disturbed minds to be set straight.
Please place laughter, joy, peace, thanksgiving, and songs of
praise to You Lord,
in the lives, minds, hearts, and homes of those who may read or
hear these words.

Please bless my mind and heart, body and soul.
Please allow me and my work to be a blessing to Your fold.

Please keep me ever so humble, so that I may forever be used by You.
When You say move, please reveal to me what You want me to do.
When You say be still, please let me hold my peace so You may have Your way.
When You say speak, please cause me to say exactly what You tell me to say.

Please help me to journey on in Thy name.
Please guide my footsteps along the way.
I am depending and trusting completely in You Dear Lord.
In the name of Thy precious and wonderful Son, Jesus, I pray.
Thank You my Lord.

Amen.

Not My Might - But His

(The Mighty Hand of God)

Nothing and
no one is
strong
enough
to hold
me down,

when my God
is holding
me up . . .

My God lifts me
above
all circumstances ! ! !

My God - - I Don't Leave Home Without Him!

My Lord is
in complete control
of EVERY situation.

And because He is
my Finisher,
everything is ALWAYS
Well Done! ! !

To: Janice,

God saw us through it all, dearest cousin, and He will continue to protect and guide us.

Love

[illegible]

June 99